Whispering in God's Ear

To Lewis
for whom the world is full of wonder

WHISPERING IN GOD'S EAR

'An Inspired Collection of
Poetry for Children'

Compiled by
ALAN MACDONALD

Illustrations by
SUSIE POOLE

LI⦿N
CHILDREN'S

A Lion Children's Book
an imprint of
Lion Hudson plc
Mayfield House, 256 Banbury Road,
Oxford OX2 7DH, England
www.lionhudson.com
ISBN 0 7459 3672 5

First edition 1994
First paperback edition 1996
10 9 8 7 6 5 4

14/3/05

A catalogue record for this book is available
from the British Library

Printed and bound in Great Britain
by Cox & Wyman Ltd, Reading

Contents

Introduction

Oh I have just had such a lovely dream!
And then I woke,
And all the dream went out like kettle steam,
Or chimney smoke.

ELEANOR FARJEON

Ever had a dream like that? One moment you are there,
and it's amazing and as real as grass, then suddenly you
wake up in your bed and the dream has melted away. All
that's left is a half-memory, a warm shiver inside. If only
you could close your eyes and be back again in the dream!

Poems are a bit like trying to capture dreams on paper.
Something flits through your mind and you try to write it
down before it goes away. Sometimes you manage it,
sometimes you don't. For me, the best poems are the ones
which preserve that first spark or shiver you felt when
you first thought of them.

Then again poems are also like secrets. They are small
treasures that you can come back to look at time and
again, perhaps with a meaning that is special to you and
nobody else.

I sometimes wonder what I would say to God if we met.
I'd probably start by asking a billion and one questions:
how did he think up the world? why are there maggots?
where do all my pens go?—that sort of thing. Then, I hope,
we might get onto other things, like dreams and secrets.

That's where the idea for the title of this book *Whispering
in God's Ear* came from. I imagined a collection of poems
that you might want to share with God when he has a
quiet moment.

Making the selection was the hardest part. There are poems of all kinds in here: poems about snow and rain, cats and Christmas, friends and strangers, songs and stories, hopes and heaven.

In choosing them I've had two things in mind. First, as a Christian, I wanted a special collection, in which all the poems fit into a biblical view of God and the world around us. Many are by poets who have (or had) a faith of their own. Others are there because they say something which Christians can nod their heads to. Secondly, the poems I've chosen are the kind I immediately wanted someone else to share—I thought they were worth whispering in somebody's ear.

I hope there are some dreams and secrets in here for you.

ALAN MACDONALD

God's Garden

IN THE BEGINNING

And God stepped out on space,
And he looked around and said:
I'm lonely—
I'll make me a world.

As far as the eye of God could see
Darkness covered everything,
Blacker than a hundred midnights
Down in a cypress swamp.

Then God smiled,
And the light broke,
And the darkness rolled up on one side,
And the light stood shining on the other,
And God said: That's good!

JAMES WELDON JOHNSON FROM 'THE SONG OF CREATION'

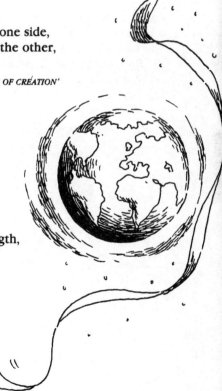

SPELL OF THE EARTH

I am the round of the globe,
The seas are my green robe,
I am where all plants grow
And the trees know

From me they draw their strength,
From me all stems find length.
I am rich in countless ways,
All footsteps give me praise.

ELIZABETH JENNINGS

PIPPA'S SONG

The year's at the spring,
And day's at the morn;
Morning's at seven;
The hill-side's dew-pearled;
The lark's on the wing;
The snail's on the thorn:
God's in his heaven—
All's right with the world!

ROBERT BROWNING

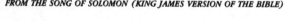

FOR LO, THE WINTER IS PAST

For, lo, the winter is past,
the rain is over and gone,
The flowers appear on the earth;
the time of the singing of birds is come,
and the voice of the turtle is heard in our land;
The fig tree putteth forth her green figs,
and the vines with the tender grape give a good smell.

FROM THE SONG OF SOLOMON (KING JAMES VERSION OF THE BIBLE)

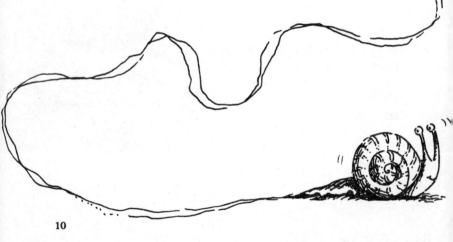

WINTER WALK

I wish I were my son again,
The first in all the world to know
The cornflake crunch of frosted grass
Beside the polar paving stones,
Beneath the drip of liquid light
From watercolour winter suns.

ADRIAN PLASS

FROST

Each blade of grass like a rapier
Makes the crisp blue sky look dull.
Fields of icy stalagmites.
It is the frost which
No leaf,
No stick,
It is the frost which no blade can deny.

JOEL STICKLEY (AGED 10)

TO A SNOWFLAKE

What heart could have thought you?
Past our devisal
(O filigree petal!)
Fashioned so purely,
Fragilely, surely,
From what Paradisal
Imagineless metal,
Too costly for cost?
Who hammered you, wrought you,
From argentine* vapour?—'God was my shaper.

Passing surmisal,
He hammered, He wrought me,
From curled silver vapour,
To lust of His mind:—
Thou couldst not have thought me!
So purely, so palely,
Tinily, surely,
Mightily, frailly,
Insculped and embossed,
With His hammer of wind,
And His graver of frost.'

FRANCIS THOMPSON

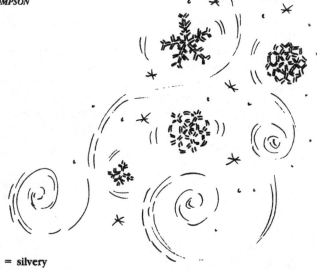

* argentine = silvery

12

AT SUNSET

God is at the anvil, beating out the sun;
Where the molten metal spills,
At his forge among the hills
He has hammered out the glory of a day that's done.

God is at the anvil, welding golden bars;
In the scarlet-streaming flame
He is fashioning a frame
For the shimmering silver beauty of the evening stars.

LEW SARETT

ESCAPE AT BEDTIME

The lights from the parlour and kitchen shone out
Through the blinds and the windows and bars;
And high overhead and all moving about,
There were thousands of millions of stars.
There ne'er were such thousands of leaves on a tree,
Nor of people in church or the Park,
As the crowds of the stars that looked down upon me,
And that glittered and winked in the dark.

The Dog, and the Plough, and the Hunter, and all,
And the star of the sailor, and Mars,
These shone in the sky, and the pail by the wall
Would be half full of water and stars.
They saw me at last, and they chased me with cries,
And they soon had me packed into bed;
But the glory kept shining and bright in my eyes,
And the stars going round in my head.

ROBERT LOUIS STEVENSON

THE WIND AND THE MOON

Said the Wind to the Moon, 'I will blow you out;
You stare
In the air
Like a ghost in a chair,
Always looking what I am about;
I hate to be watched; I will blow you out.'

The Wind blew hard, and out went the Moon.
So, deep
On a heap
Of clouds to sleep,
Down lay the Wind, and slumbered soon—
Muttering low, 'I've done for that Moon.'

He turned in his bed; she was there again!
On high,
In the sky,
With her one ghost eye,
The Moon shone white and alive and plain,
Said the Wind, 'I will blow you out again.'...

He flew in a rage; he danced and blew;
But in vain
Was the pain
Of his bursting brain;
For still the broader the Moon-scrap grew
The broader he swelled his big cheeks and blew.

Slowly she grew, till she filled the night,
And shone
On her throne
In the sky alone,
A matchless, wonderful, silvery light,
Radiant and lovely, the Queen of the night.

Said the Wind, 'What a marvel of power am I!
With my breath,
Good faith,
I blew her to death—
First blew her away right out of the sky—
Then blew her right in; what strengh have I!'

But the Moon she knew nothing about the affair;
For high
In the sky,
With her one white eye,
Motionless, miles above the air,
She had never heard the great Wind blare.

GEORGE MACDONALD FROM 'THE WIND AND THE MOON'

RAIN

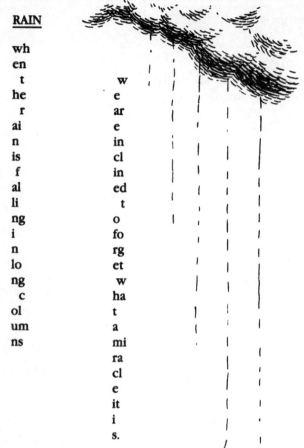

wh
en
t
he
r
ai
n
is
f
al
li
ng
i
n
lo
ng
c
ol
um
ns

w
e
ar
e
in
cl
in
ed
t
o
fo
rg
et
w
ha
t
a
mi
ra
cl
e
it
i
s.

GEORGE MACBETH

A SLASH OF BLUE

A slash of Blue—
A sweep of Gray—
Some scarlet patches on the way,
Compose an Evening Sky—
A little purple—slipped between
Some Ruby Trousers hurried on—
A Wave of Gold—
A Bank of Day—
This just makes out the Morning Sky.

EMILY DICKINSON

WHAT IS PINK?

What is pink? A rose is pink
By the fountain's brink.
What is red? A poppy's red
In its barley bed.
What is blue? The sky is blue
Where the clouds float through.
What is white? A swan is white
Sailing in the light.
What is yellow? Pears are yellow,
Rich and ripe and mellow.
What is green? The grass is green,
With small flowers between.
What is violet? Clouds are violet
In the summer twilight.
What is orange? Why, an orange,
Just an orange!

CHRISTINA ROSSETTI

THANKS

Thank you very much indeed,
River, for your waving reed;
Hollyhocks, for budding knobs;
Foxgloves, for your velvet fobs;
Pansies, for your silky cheeks;
Chaffinches, for singing beaks;
Spring, for wood anemones
Near the mossy toes of trees;
Summer, for the fruited pear,
Yellowing crab, and cherry fare;
Autumn, for the bearded load,
Hazelnuts along the road;
Winter, for the fairy-tale,
Spitting log and bouncing hail.

But, blest Father, high above,
All these joys are from Thy love;
And Your children everywhere,
Born in palace, lane, or square,
Cry with voices all agreed,
'Thank you very much indeed.'

NORMAN GALE

PIED BEAUTY

Glory be to God for dappled things—
For skies of couple-colour as a brinded cow;
For rose-moles all in stipple upon trout that swim;
Fresh-firecoal chestnut-falls; finches' wings;
Landscapes plotted and pieced—fold, fallow, and plough;
And all trades, their gear and tackle and trim.

All things counter, original, spare, strange;
Whatever is fickle, freckled (who knows how?)
With swift, slow; sweet, sour; adazzle, dim;
He fathers-forth whose beauty is past change:
Praise him.

GERARD MANLEY HOPKINS

GIVING THANKS GIVING THANKS

Giving thanks giving thanks
for rain and rainbows
sun and sunsets
cats and catbirds
larks and larkspur

giving thanks giving thanks
for cows and cowslips
eggs and eggplants
stars and starlings
dogs and dogwood

giving thanks giving thanks
for watercress on riverbanks
for necks and elbows knees and shanks
for towers basins pools and tanks
for pumps and handles lifts and cranks

giving thanks giving thanks
for ropes and coils and braids and hanks
for jobs and jokes and plots and pranks
for whistles bells and plinks and clanks
giving giving giving *thanks*

EVE MERRIAM

THE WORLD

Great, wide, beautiful, wonderful World,
With the wonderful water round you curled,
And the wonderful grass upon your breast—
World, you are beautifully dressed.

The wonderful air is over me,
And the wonderful wind is shaking the tree,
It walks on the water, and whirls the mills,
And talks to itself on the tops of the hills.

You friendly Earth, how far do you go,
With the wheatfields that nod and the rivers that flow,
With cities and gardens, and cliffs, and isles,
And people upon you for thousands of miles?

Ah, you are so great, and I am so small,
I tremble to think of you, World, at all;
And yet, when I said my prayers today,
A whisper inside me seemed to say,
'You are more than the Earth, though you are such a dot;
You can love and think, and the Earth cannot'.

WILLIAM BRIGHTY RANDS

An Ark of Animals

AN ARK OF ANIMALS

If animals lived in houses
Where do you think they'd all go?
Does a duck ever dream of a semi in Cheam
Or a bull of a small bungalow?

Would a horse be at home in the Hilton Hotel
With a bale of hay in the bath?
Or a cat keep a cottage in Cornwall
With a neat crazy-paving path?

Would a goat live afloat on a houseboat,
Giving parties for otters and owls?
Can you picture a pig in a palace
Eating oysters from silverware bowls?

Would a vole and a mole share a villa in France
Drinking cocktails and catching the sun?
Or a fox have the roam of a stately home
Where he'd go hunting farmers for fun?

Would a deer find it queer in a castle
With a butler to answer the door?
Would a bat's habitat be a high-rise flat
To hang out on the ninety-third floor?

But animals don't live in houses,
They have forests and fields to run free
And perhaps it's as well since they might make a smell,
And there wouldn't be room for me!

ALAN MACDONALD

THE NAMING OF THE ANIMALS

What would you call this animal, Adam?
He's proud and he prowls and he roars
He's stronger than anyone else I made
His coat is the colour of straw.

What would you call this animal, Adam?
Her neck stretches up to the trees
She has four terribly spindley legs
And four very knobbly knees.

What would you call this animal, Adam?
With a tube instead of a nose
His ears are like clothes on a washing line
And he hurrumphs wherever he goes.

What would you call this animal, Adam?
Her skin is as tough as old rope
A horn sticks up on the end of her nose
And mud is her favourite soap.

What would you call this animal, Adam?
He swoops from the sky for his lunch
He knits his own house from branches and leaves
And swallows a mouse with a crunch.

What would you call this human, Adam?
I made her to be your best friend
Take her and love her as if she was you
And stay by her side 'til the end.

STEVE TURNER

PRAISE GOD FOR THE ANIMALS

Praise God for the animals
for the colours of them,
for the spots and stripes of them,
for the patches and plains of them,
their claws and paws.

LYNN WARREN

LITTLE TROTTY WAGTAIL

Little trotty wagtail, he went in the rain,
And tittering, tottering sideways he ne'er got straight again,
He stooped to get a worm, and looked up to catch a fly,
And then he flew away ere his feathers they were dry.

Little trotty wagtail, he waddled in the mud,
And left his little footmarks, trample where he would.
He waddled in the water-pudge, and waggle went his tail,
And chirrup up his wings to dry upon the garden rail.

Little trotty wagtail, you nimble all about,
And in the dimpling water-pudge you waddle in and out;
Your home is nigh at hand, and in the warm pigsty,
So, little Master Wagtail, I'll bid you a good-bye.

JOHN CLARE

THREE LITTLE OWLS WHO SANG HYMNS

There were three little owls in a wood
who sang hymns whenever they could;
What the words were about
One could never make out,
But one felt it was doing them good.

ANON

23

THE OWL

When cats run home and light is come,
And dew is cold upon the ground,
And the far-off stream is dumb,
And the whirring sail goes round,
And the whirring sail goes round;
Alone and warming his five wits,
The white owl in the belfry sits.

When merry milkmaids click the latch,
And rarely smells the new-mown hay,
And the cock hath sung beneath the thatch
Twice or thrice his roundelay,*
Twice or thrice his roundelay;
Alone and warming his five wits,
The white owl in the belfry sits.

ALFRED, LORD TENNYSON

SEAL LULLABY

Oh hush thee my baby, the night is behind us,
And black are the waters that sparkled so green.
The moon, o'er the combers, looks downward to find us
At rest in the hollows that rustle between.
Where billow meets billow, there soft be thy pillow;
Ah weary wee flipperling, curl at thy ease!
The storm shall not wake thee, nor sharks overtake thee,
Asleep in the arms of the slow-swinging seas.

RUDYARD KIPLING

* roundelay = song

A FRIEND IN THE GARDEN

He is not John the gardener
And yet the whole day long
Employs himself most usefully,
The flower beds among.

He is not Tom the pussy cat,
And yet the other day
With stealthy stride and glistening eye,
He crept upon his prey.

He is not Dash the dear old dog,
And yet, perhaps, if you
Took pains with him and petted him,
You'd come to love him too.

He's not a blackbird, though he chirps,
And though he was once black;
And now he wears a loose grey coat,
All wrinkled on the back.

He's got a very dirty face,
And very shining eyes;
He sometimes comes and sits indoors;
He looks—and p'r'aps is—wise.

But in a sunny flower bed
He has a fixed abode;
He eats the things that eat my plants—
He is a friendly TOAD.

JULIANA HORATIA EWING

CAT

The fat cat on the mat
may seem to dream
of nice mice that suffice
for him, or cream;
but free, maybe,
walks in thought
unbowed, proud, where loud
roared and fought
his kin, lean and slim,
or deep in den
in the East feasted on beasts
and tender men.

The giant lion with iron
claw in paw,
and huge ruthless tooth
in gory jaw;
the pard dark-starred
fleet upon feet
that oft soft from aloft
leaps on his meat
where woods loom in gloom—
far now they be,
fierce and free,
and tamed is he;
but fat cat on the mat
kept as a pet,
he does not forget.

J.R.R. TOLKIEN

26

CAT

Cat!
Scat!
Atter her, atter her,
Sleeky flatterer,
Spitfire chatterer,
Scatter her, scatter her
Off her mat!
Wuff!
Wuff!
Treat her rough!
Git her, git her,
Whiskery spitter!
Catch her, catch her,
Green-eyed scratcher!
Slathery
Slithery
Hisser,
Don't miss her!
Run till you're dithery,
Hithery
Thithery
Pfitts! Pfitts!
How she spits!
Spitch! Spatch!
Can't she scratch!
Scritching the bark
Of the sycamore-tree,
She's reached her ark
And's hissing at me
Pfitts! Pfitts!
Wuff! Wuff!
Scat,
Cat!
That's
That!

ELEANOR FARJEON

MY CAT JEOFFRY

For I will consider my cat Jeoffry.

For he is the servant of the Living God, duly and daily
   serving him...

For first he looks upon his fore-paws to see if they
   are clean.

For secondly he kicks up behind to clear away there.

For thirdly he works it upon stretch with the fore-paws
   extended.

For fourthly he sharpens his paws by wood.

For fifthly he washes himself.

For sixthly he rolls upon wash.

For seventhly he fleas himself, that he may not be
   interrupted upon the beat.

For eighthly he rubs himself against a post.

For ninthly he looks up for his instructions.

For tenthly he goes in quest of food.

For having considered God and himself he will consider
   his neighbour

For if he meets another cat he will kiss her in kindness...

For he will not do destruction if he is well-fed, neither will
   he spit without provocation.

For he purrs in thankfulness, when God tells him he's a
   good Cat.

CHRISTOPHER SMART

THE TIGER

Tiger! Tiger! burning bright
In the forests of the night,
What immortal hand or eye
Could frame thy fearful symmetry?

In what distant deeps or skies
Burned the fire of thine eyes?
On what wings dare he aspire?
What the hand dare seize the fire?

And what shoulder, and what art,
Could twist the sinews of thy heart?
And when thy heart began to beat,
What dread hand? And what dread feet?

What the hammer? What the chain?
In what furnace was thy brain?
What the anvil? What dread grasp
Dare its deadly terrors clasp?

When the stars threw down their spears,
And watered heaven with their tears,
Did he smile his work to see?
Did he who made the Lamb make thee?

Tiger! Tiger! burning bright
In the forests of the night,
What immortal hand or eye
Dare frame thy fearful symmetry?

WILLIAM BLAKE

THE ELEPHANT

The magnificent head reared in protest,
At the poacher's nearing,
The leathery skin wrinkled and strong,
The little beady eyes
Watchful for his family,
Swaying and stumbling through the trees,
The Royal beast comes,
A majestic move, a swift strong stride
Describes this enormous animal,
The satellite ears alert and listening,
Listening for the sound of feet approaching near.
This true animal is purely the crest of the jungle.

The tusks await the moment of burning,
The evidence of crime,
Symbol of the elephants
Sacrificed for man's selfishness,
A vague memory
Of the beasts who died in pain.
The shining mists of ivory,
Echoing the shouts of a bull elephant,
Who died in vain.
The soft burn and then
A blaze,
Honouring our animal's death.
Sadness and sorrow,
Emptiness and the hollow
Feeling of despair.

KATEY SCOTT (AGED 11)

HE WAS A RAT

He was a rat, and she was a rat,
And down in one hole they did dwell,
And both were as black as a witch's cat,
And they loved one another well.

He had a tail, and she had a tail,
Both long and curling and fine;
And each said, 'Yours is the finest tail
In the world, excepting mine.'

He smelt the cheese, and she smelt the cheese,
And they both pronounced it good;
And both remarked it would greatly add
To the charms of their daily food.

So he ventured out, and she ventured out,
And I saw them go with pain,
For what befell them I never can tell,
For they never came back again.

ANON

THE LONG GIRAFFE

The long giraffe
emits no laugh
when forced to take
an evening bath
His legs don't fold
his ears get cold
his dusty frame
of patchwork gold
can only guess
the happiness
of being clean
from jungly mess

And ones that creep
and some that cheep
can float, then pierce
the silver deep
And those that roar
plus beasts that gore
can feel the wet
seep through each pore.
Whilst those with fins
enjoy gloss skins
giraffe is moist
below his shins

But I propose
that nothing glows
quite like his beam
ing gleaming toes.

STEWART HENDERSON

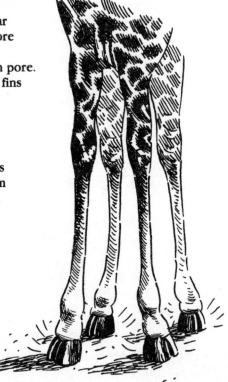

THE DRAGON SPEAKS

Now I keep watch on the gold in my rock cave
In a country of stones: old, deplorable dragon,
Watching my hoard. In winter night the gold
Freezes through tough scales my cold belly;
Jagged crowns, cruelly twisted rings,
Icy and knobb'd, are the old dragon's bed.

Often I wish I had not eaten my wife
(Though worm grows not to dragon till he eats worm).
She could have helped me, watch and watch about,
Guarding the gold; the gold would have been safer.
I could uncoil my tired body and take
Sometimes a little sleep when she was watching.

Last night under the moonset a fox barked,
Startled me; then I knew I had been sleeping.
Often an owl flying over the country of stones
Startles me; then I think that I must have slept,
Only a moment. That very moment a Man
Might have come from the towns to steal my gold...

They have no pity for the old, lugubrious dragon.
Lord that made the dragon, grant me thy peace,
But say not that I should give up the gold,
Nor move, nor die. Others would have the gold.
Kill rather, Lord, the Men and the other dragons;
Then I can sleep; go when I will to drink.

C.S. LEWIS FROM 'THE DRAGON SPEAKS'

INSECTS

Have you ever seen a bug in a bed,
Or a spider in a bath?
Have you ever seen a fly read a book,
Or a centipede laugh?
Have you ever seen a butterfly swim,
Or a ladybird cry?
Have you ever seen a bee dance,
Or a caterpillar sigh?
And because these creatures are very clever,
They will live with us forever.

HELEN ARCHER (AGED 8)

THE BUTTERFLY IN CHURCH

Butterfly, butterfly, why come you here?
This is no bower for you;
Go, sip the honey-drop sweet and clear,
Or bathe in the morning dew.

This is the place to think of heaven,
This is the place to pray;
You have no sins to be forgiven—
Butterfly, go away!

WILLIAM COWPER

THE DONKEY

When fishes flew and forest walked
And figs grew upon thorn,
Some moment when the moon was blood
Then surely I was born;

With monstrous head and sickening cry
And ears like errant wings,
The devil's walking parody
On all four-footed things.

The tattered outlaw of the earth,
Of ancient crooked will;
Starve, scourge, deride me: I am dumb,
I keep my secrets still.

Fools! For I also had my hour;
One far fierce hour and sweet:
There was a shout about my ears,
And palms before my feet.

G.K. CHESTERTON

A World in my Head

FRIGHTENING FATHER

'Quick! My monster mask!' I said to Mum
when I heared Dad's key in the lock.
I hided my face so a horrible shock
would tremble his teeth and wobble his tum.

I crouched on my bed like a leopard on a rock
and bemagined the cheekiest name to shout.
When Dad walked by, I jumped out
and said, 'Garr! You dirty old frying sock!'

'Help! A monster!' he cried as he fell on the floor.
I jumped on his back and banged him a boff.
'It's just me, Dad!' I said and I took my mask off
so he wouldn't be frightened no more.

'Oh you sinful singlet! You smouldering smock!
You wicked and worsted waistcoat!' he said.
And he tickled my tummy with his hairy head.
'Mercy!' I said. 'You dirty old frying sock!'

ANDREW LANSDOWN

I'M NOBODY! WHO ARE YOU?

I'm Nobody! Who are you?
Are you—Nobody—Too?
Then there's a pair of us?
Don't tell! they'd advertise—you know!

How dreary—to be—Somebody!
How public—like a Frog—
To tell one's name—the livelong June—
To an admiring Bog!

EMILY DICKINSON

MY BATH

My bath is the ocean
and I am a continent
with hills and valleys
and earthquakes and storms.
I put the two mountain peaks of my knees
underwater and bring them up again.

Our earth was like that—
great churnings and splashings,
and continents appearing and disappearing.
Only you, O God, know about it all,
and understand and take care
of all creation.

MADELEINE L'ENGLE

NIGHT

Night like the black hole
Giant shadows flitting.
An orange magical ball,
Disappearing behind the horizon.
My courage topples,
As I begin to shiver.
I spot another shadow
Hover by the washing line.
The orange sun rises,
It's the warm familiar morning.

NAOMI MACDONALD (AGED 11)

QUESTIONS AT NIGHT

Why
Is the sky?

What starts the thunder overhead?
Who makes the crashing noise?
Are the angels falling out of bed?
Are they breaking all their toys?

Why does the sun go down so soon?
Why do the night-clouds crawl
Hungrily up to the new-laid moon
And swallow it, shell and all?

If there's a Bear among the stars,
As all the people say,
Won't he jump over those pasture-bars
And drink up the Milky Way?

Does every star that happens to fall
Turn into a firefly?
Can't it ever get back to Heaven at all?
And why
Is the sky?

LOUIS UNTERMEYER

THE PESSIMIST

Nothing to do but work,
Nothing to eat but food,
Nothing to wear but clothes
To keep one from going nude.

Nothing to breathe but air,
Quick as a flash 'tis gone;
Nowhere to fall but off,
Nowhere to stand but on.

Nothing to comb but hair,
Nowhere to sleep but in bed,
Nothing to weep but tears,
Nothing to bury but dead.

Nothing to sing but songs,
Ah, well, alas! alack!
Nowhere to go but out,
Nowhere to come but back.

Nothing to see but sights,
Nothing to quench but thirst,
Nothing to have but what we've got;
Thus thro' life we are cursed.

Nothing to strike but a gait;*
Everything moves that goes.
Nothing at all but common sense
Can ever withstand these woes.

BEN KING

* gait = way of walking

TOPSY-TURVEY-WORLD

If the butterfly courted the bee,
And the owl the porcupine;
If churches were built in the sea,
And three times one was nine;
If the pony rode his master,
If the buttercups ate the cows,
If the cat had the dire disaster
To be worried, sir, by the mouse;
If mamma, sir, sold the baby
To a gipsy for half a pound;
If a gentleman, sir, was a lady—
The world would have Upside-Downed!
If any or all of these wonders
Should ever come about,
I should not consider them blunders,
For I should be Inside-Out!

WILLIAM BRIGHTY RANDS

FRIENDS

I fear it's very wrong of me
And yet I must admit
When someone offers friendship
I want the *whole* of it.
I don't want everybody else
To share my friends with me.
At least, I want *one* special one,
Who, indisputably

  Likes me much more than all the rest,
Who's always on my side.
Who never cares what others say,
Who lets me come and hide
Within his shadow, in his house—
It doesn't matter where—
Who let's me simply be myself,
Who's always, *always* there.

ELIZABETH JENNINGS

40

NOT LIKE US

funny things foreigners
with their funny clothes
and funny languages
and funny food
(even eat horses some of them)
funny
not like us

funny things women
with their funny make-up
and funny clothes
and funny emotions
(you never know where you are with them)
funny
not like us

funny things neighbours
with their funny wallpaper
and funny house smells
and funny taste in music
(which drifts over when you're in the garden)
funny
not like us

funny things strangers
with their funny habits
and funny attitudes
and funny children
(who they always take to the shops to smack)
funny
not like us
me and my mates
we're normal

MIKE STARKEY

cHILD pRODIGY

i go to a special needs school
does that mean that im special
im just after nine and like making dinosaurs
i use words which are called swearing
it makes the teachers cross.
its my way of getting my own back
funny that isnt it
my own back
do you have your own back
i do

look

see its at the front now
when i swear
im saying something else inside
teachers notice me when i swear
it makes the others in our class laugh
my fathers girlfriend is having a baby
i hope its a girl
cos he doesnt like boys
i wonder if shell be like me
special

STEWART HENDERSON

THE TIGER

When something makes me angry
When something drives me wild,
A tiger creeps inside my skin
Who wants to be a child.

His eyes are big as saucers,
His hands are sharp with claws,
He prowls around our sofa
And scratches on the doors.

He kicks my little brother
And takes away his toys,
He snarls at my mother
With a growling, spitting noise.

He doesn't eat his brussel sprouts,
He throws them on the floor,
He leaves the table in a rage
And slams the kitchen door.

He paces through the flower beds,
He slinks into the shed,
He chases out a sleeping cat
—And gets sent up to bed.

He sneaks under the covers
And licks his dirty paws,
He yawns and curls up on my bed
And sleeps with tiger snores.

When I'm tired of being angry
When I've finished being wild
The tiger slips out from my skin
And I wake up—a child.

ALAN MACDONALD

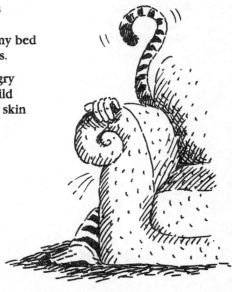

CERTAINTY

I never saw a Moor—
I never saw the Sea—
Yet I know how the Heather looks
And what a Billow be.

I never spoke with God
Nor visited in Heaven—
Yet certain am I of the spot
As if the Checks were given.

EMILY DICKINSON

HEAVEN

Heaven is
The place where
Happiness is
Everywhere.
Animals
And birds sing—
As does
Everything.
To each stone,
'How-do-you-do?'
'Well! And you?'

LANGSTON HUGHES

THE THANKS OF A BOY

God, who created me
Nimble and light of limb,
In three elements free,
To run, to ride, to swim;
Not when the sense is dim,
But now from the heart of joy,
I would remember him:
Take the thanks of a boy.

HENRY CHARLES BEECHING

THE SMILE

My mother prayed that I should have the sweet tooth.
My father said that I should have the big fist.
And life, lingering somewhere by,
Smiled on me, giving me neither.

R.S. THOMAS

All God's Children

WHERE DID YOU COME FROM, BABY DEAR?

Where did you come from, baby dear?
Out of the everywhere into here.

Where did you get your eyes so blue?
Out of the sky as I came through.

What makes the light in them sparkle and spin?
Some of the starry spikes left in.

Where did you get that little tear?
I found it waiting when I got here.

What makes your forehead so smooth and high?
A soft hand stroked it as I went by.

What makes your cheek like a warm white rose?
I saw something better than anyone knows.

Whence that three-cornered smile of bliss?
Three angels gave me at once a kiss.

Where did you get this pearly ear?
God spoke, and it came out to hear.

Where did you get those arms and hands?
Love made itself into hooks and bands.

Feet, whence did you come, you darling things?
From the same box as the cherubs' wings.

How did they all just come to be you?
God thought about me, and so I grew.

But how did you come to us, you dear?
God thought about you, and so I am here.

GEORGE MACDONALD

GOOD AND BAD CHILDREN

Children, you are very little,
And your bones are very brittle;
If you would grow great and stately,
You must try to walk sedately.

You must still be bright and quiet,
And content with simple diet;
And remain, through all bewild'ring,
Innocent and honest children.

Happy hearts and happy faces,
Happy play in grassy places—
That was how, in ancient ages,
Children grew to kings and sages.

But the unkind and the unruly,
And the sort who eat unduly,
They must never hope for glory—
Theirs is quite a different story!

Cruel children, crying babies,
All grow up as geese and gabies,
Hated, as their age increases,
By their nephews and their nieces.

ROBERT LOUIS STEVENSON

THERE WAS A NAUGHTY BOY

There was a naughty boy,
A naughty boy was he,
He would not stop at home,
He could not quiet be—
He took
In his knapsack
A book
Full of vowels
And a shirt
With some towels,
A slight cap
For night cap,
A hair brush,
Comb ditto,
New stockings—
For old ones
Would split O!
This knapsack
Tight at 's back
He rivetted close
And followed his nose
To the North,
To the North,
And followed his nose
To the North.

There was a naughty boy,
And a naughty boy was he,
He ran away to Scotland
The people for to see—
There he found
That the ground
Was as hard,
That a yard
Was as long,
That a song
Was as merry,
That a cherry
Was as red—
That lead
Was as weighty
That fourscore
Was as eighty,
That a door
Was as wooden
As in England—
So he stood in his shoes
And he wondered,
He wondered,
He stood in his shoes
And he wondered.

JOHN KEATS

48

FRED

Fred likes creatures
And has a lot of 'em.
Bees don't sting him,
He's got a pot of 'em,
Little round velvety bodies they are
Making honey in Fred's jam-jar.

Fred likes creatures
Hedgehogs don't prickle him,
They flatten their quills
And scarcely tickle him,
But lie with their pointed snouts on his palm,
And their beady eyes are perfectly calm.

Fred likes creatures
The nestling fallen out
Of the tree-top
With magpie callin' out
Where? Where? Where? contented lingers
In the round nest of Fred's thick fingers.

Fred likes creatures
Nothing's queer to him,
Ferrets, tortoises,
Newts are dear to him,
The lost wild rabbit comes to his hand
As to a burrow in friendly land.

Fred *eats* rabbit
Like any glutton, too
Fred eats chicken
And beef and mutton too.
Moral? None. No more to be said.
Than Fred likes creatures, and creatures like Fred.

ELEANOR FARJEON

THE REST OF THE DAY'S YOUR OWN

One day when I was out of work a job I went to seek,
To be a farmer's boy.
At last I found an easy job at half a crown a week,
To be a farmer's boy.
The farmer said, 'I think I've got the very job for you;
Your duties will be light, for this is all you've got to do:
Rise at three every morn, milk the cow with the
    crumpled horn,
Feed the pigs, clean the sty, teach the pigeons the
    way to fly,
Plough the fields, mow the hay, help the cocks and
    hens to lay,
Sow the seeds, tend the crops, chase the flies from the
    turnip tops.
Clean the knives, black the shoes, scrub the kitchen and
    sweep the flues,
Help the wife, wash the pots, grow cabbages and car*rots*,
Make the beds, dust the coals, mend the gramophone,
And then if there's no more work to do, the rest of the
    day's your own.'

I scratched my head and thought it would be absolutely
    prime
To be a farmer's boy.
The farmer said, 'Of course you'll have to do some
    overtime,
When you're a farmer's boy.' Said he, 'The duties that I've
given you, you'll be
    quickly through,
So I've been thinking of a few more things that you can do:
Skim the milk, make the cheese, chop the meat
    for the sausa*gees*,
Bath the kids, mend their clothes, use your dial*
    to scare the crows,
In the milk, put the chalk, shave the knobs off the
    pickled pork,
Shoe the horse, break the coal, take the cat for his
    midnight stroll,

Cook the food, scrub the stairs, teach the parrot
   to say his prayers,
Roast the joint, bake the bread, shake the feathers
   up in the bed,
When the wife's got the gout, rub her funny bone,
And then if there's no more work to do, the rest of
   the day's your own.'

I thought it was a shame to take the money, you can bet,
To be a farmer's boy.
And so I wrote my duties down in case I should forget
I was a farmer's boy.
It took all night to write 'em down, I didn't go to bed,
But somehow I got all mixed up, and this is how they read:
Rise at three, every morn, milk the hen with the
   crumpled horn,
Scrub the wife every day, teach the nanny goat how to lay,
Shave the cat, mend the cheese, fit the tights on
   the sausa*gees*,
Bath the pigs, break the pots, boil the kids with a
   few car*rots*,
Roast the horse, dust the bread, put the cocks and hens
   to bed,
Boots and shoes, black with chalk, shave the hair on
   the pickled pork,
All the rest I forgot, somehow it had flown,
But I got the sack this morning, so that the rest of my life's
   my own.

ANON

• dial = face

AN OLD WOMAN OF THE ROADS

Oh, to have a little house!
To own the hearth and stool and all!
The heaped-up sods upon the fire,
The pile of turf against the wall.

To have a clock with weights and chains
And pendulum swinging up and down,
A dresser filled with shining delph,*
Speckled and white and blue and brown.

I could be busy all the day
Clearing and sweeping hearth and floor,
And fixing on their shelf again
My blue and white and speckled store.

I could be quiet there at night,
Beside the fire and by myself,
Sure of a bed, and loth to leave
The ticking clock and the shining delph.

Och! but I'm weary of mist and dark,
And roads where there's never a house or bush,
And tired I am of bog and road,
And the crying wind and the lonesome hush.

And I am praying to God on high,
And I am praying him night and day,
For a little house, a house of my own—
Out of the wind's and the rain's way.

PADRAIC COLUM

* delph = Dutch pottery

THE PEDLAR'S CARAVAN

I wish I lived in a caravan,
With a horse to drive, like a pedlar-man!
Where he comes from nobody knows,
Or where he goes to, but on he goes!

His caravan has windows two,
And a chimney of tin, that the smoke come through;
He has a wife, with a baby brown,
And they go riding from town to town.

Chairs to mend, and delf to sell!
He clashes the basins like a bell;
Tea-trays, baskets ranged in order,
Plates, with alphabets round the border!

The roads are brown, and the sea is green,
But his house is like a bathing-machine;
The world is round, and he can ride,
Rumble and slash, to the other side!

With the pedlar-man I should like to roam,
And write a book when I came home;
All the people would read my book,
Just like the Travels of Captain Cook!

WILLIAM BRIGHTY RANDS

HERE'S THE REVEREND RUNDLE

Here's the Reverend Rundle
His gear in a bundle,
He has a dog
He has a sled
And thousands of stories
In his head
And coloured pictures
Of the Holy Scriptures
To show, show
The Indians red
Who had picture and story
And saints in glory
And a heavenly throne
Of their very own
But were so well-bred
That they met him like a brother
And they loved each other
It was said,
The Reverend Rundle
And the Indians red
And through the Rockies
They watched him go
Over the ice
And under the snow—
But this was a very long, long, long
Time ago.

They loved him from
His heels to his hat
As he rode on the rough
Or walked on the flat
Whether he stood
Or whether he sat,
The Reverend Rundle
His gear in a bundle
And as well as that
His favourite cat
Warm in a poke
Of his sealskin cloak
For fear some son
Of a hungry gun
Ate her for supper
In Edmonton
And they loved each other
It was said,
The Reverend Rundle
And the Indians red
And through the Rockies
They watched him go
Over the ice
And under the snow—
But this was a very long ·
Time ago,
A long, long, long, long
Time ago.

CHARLES CAUSLEY

THE CLOWN

Others are noble and admired—
The ones who walk the tightrope without nets,
The one who goes inside the lion's cage,
And all the grave, audacious acrobats.
Away from fear and rage
He simply is the interval for tired

People who cannot bear
Too much excitement. They can see in him
Their own lost innocence or else their fear
(For him no metal bars or broken limb).
Have they forgotten that it takes as much
Boldness to tumble, entertain and jest
When loneliness walks tightropes in your breast
And every joke is like a wild beast's touch?

ELIZABETH JENNINGS

Grave Humour

ON LESLIE MOORE

Here lies what's left
Of Leslie Moore
No Les
No more.

ON A DENTIST

Stranger, approach this spot with gravity,
John Brown is filling his last cavity.

ON MARTHA SNELL

Poor Martha Snell, she's gone away
She would have stayed, but could not stay.
She had bad legs and a hacking cough
It was her legs that carried her off.

ON PRINCE FREDERICK

Here lies Fred
Who was alive and is dead.
Had it been his father,
I had much rather;
Had it been his brother,
Still better than another;
Had it been his sister,
No one would have missed her;
Had it been the whole generation,
Still better for the nation;
But since 'tis only Fred,
Who was alive and is dead
There's no more to be said.

People of the Book

MAKING ADAM

Then God sat down—
On the side of a hill where he could think;
By a deep, wide river he sat down;
With his head in his hands,
God thought and thought,
Till he thought, I'll make me a man!

Up from the bed of the river
God scooped the clay;
And by the bank of the river
He kneeled him down;
And there the great God Almighty
Who lit the sun and fixed it in the sky,
Who flung the stars to the most far corner of the night,
Who rounded the earth in the middle of his hand;
This great God,
Like a mammy bending over her baby,
Kneeled down in the dust
Toiling over a lump of clay
Till he shaped it in his own image;
Then into it he blew the breath of life,
And man became a living soul.
Amen. Amen.

JAMES WELDON JOHNSON, FROM 'THE CREATION'

SPARE RIB

God made de light
to shine out bright
Him call it day—and de darkness night!
Den Him call fi water
Fi separate de space
Put de sea out so
And de land inna place!
Den de Lawd was pleased at what Him do,
So next—
Him bring forth grass and every plant too!
Sun and moon and stars Him make
But—
Even den Him never tek one break!
When Him look inna de sea
Him find it bare
So Him put some fish and creatures dere.
De same ting Him sey bout de empty land
So him make livestock
And den Him make Man—
—Him create every ting on dis earth
An ME
Him make fram a spare rib!

MILLIE MURRAY

NOAH

Noah was an Admiral;
Never a one but he
Sailed for forty days and nights
With wife and children three
On such a mighty sea.

Under his tempest-battered deck
This Admiral had a zoo;
And all the creatures in the world,
He kept them, two by two—
Ant, hippo, kangaroo,

And every other beast beside,
Of every mould and make.
When tempests howled and thunder growled
How they did cower and quake
To feel the vessel shake!

But Noah was a Carpenter
Had made his ship so sound
That not a soul of crew or zoo
In all that time was drowned ·
Before they reached dry ground.

So Admiral, Keeper, Carpenter—
Now should *you* put to sea
In such a flood, it would be good
If one of these you be,
But better still—all three!

JAMES REEVES

THE ANIMALS WENT IN TWO BY TWO

The animals went in two by two,
Hurrah! Hurrah!
The animals went in two by two,
The elephant and the kangaroo,
And they all went into the ark
For to get out of the rain.

The animals went in three by three,
Hurrah! Hurrah!
The animals went in three by three,
The wasp, the ant and the bumble bee,
And they all went into the ark
For to get out of the rain.

The animals went in four by four
Hurrah! Hurrah!
The animals went in four by four,
The great hippopotamus stuck in the door,
And they all went into the ark
For to get out of the rain...

ANON

MEASLES IN THE ARK

The night it was horribly dark,
The measles broke out in the Ark;
Little Japheth, and Shem, and all the young Hams,
Were screaming at once for potatoes and clams.
And 'What shall I do,' said poor Mrs. Noah,
'All alone by myself in this terrible shower?
I know what I'll do: I'll step down in the hold,
And wake up a lioness grim and old,
And tie her close to the children's door,
And give her a ginger-cake to roar
At the top of her voice for an hour or more;
And I'll tell the children to cease their din,
Or I'll let that grim old party in,
To stop their squeazles and likewise their measles.'
She practised this with the greatest success:
She was everyone's grandmother, I guess.

SUSAN COOLIDGE

JOSHUA'S BATTLE

Joshua fit the battle of Jericho, Jericho, Jericho,
Joshua fit the battle of Jericho,
And the walls came tumbling down.

You may talk about your king of Gideon,
You may talk about your man of Saul,
But there's none like good old Joshua
At the battle of Jericho.

Up to the walls of Jericho
He marched with spear in hand.
'Go blow them ram-horns,' Joshua cried,
''Cause the battle am in my hand.'

Them the ram-horns began to blow,
Trumpets began to sound.
Joshua commanded the children to shout,
And the walls came tumbling down, that morning,
The walls came tumbling down.

Joshua fit the battle of Jericho, Jericho, Jericho,
Joshua fit the battle of Jericho,
And the walls came tumbling down.

TRADITIONAL AFRICAN AMERICAN SPIRITUAL

DAVID AND GOLIATH

Goliath rang,
an iron man:
helmet, brass,
coat of mail,
breastplate, legplates,
spear and shield.
Ten feet tall,
spearshaft wide
as any arm
on that mountainside.

I'll fight this man,
said David.
King Saul was full of doubt
but they set him up in plates of brass,
quite sure that he had breathed his last
and sent him out.

The shepherd boy
took off his mail,
took off his shield and sword.
I fought a lion with God's help,
I'm safe with just His word.
Goliath is no jackal
though he hides in a coat of mail,
and might's not right
in every fight;
I shall not fail.

Goliath looked. He stared.
He laughed. He roared.
His legplates shook,
his army cheered.

Goliath jeered.

I'll give your flesh
to the fowls of the air,
your heart
to the beasts of the field;
your liver will fill
some roaming bear
when I've wiped you
off my shield!
Where is your sword,
vile midget?
Are you really
the best they could find?
Step forward,
let's finish this quickly!
I'll grind your bones
like summer wheat
and scatter your chaff
to the wind!

But David stood.

He heard the Philistines' laughter,
he heard Goliath's jeer;
the giant's metal music rang
discordant in his ear.

He picked five stones
from a nearby stream;
swung one, flung one, stood...
it arched like Noah's rainbow
then caught the giant's head.
He fell like a dove to the mountainside.
His army scattered like chaff as they cried
Goliath's dead!

David was a shepherd boy,
Jesse's youngest son;
slew Goliath,
saved his country—
with a stone.

JUDITH NICHOLLS FROM 'DAVID AND GOLIATH'

JONAH'S LAMENT

Dark, only dark,
with only hands for eyes;
saved—for a life of touch!
Is *this* my end,
fumbling at some bony stalactite
inside this dank, rank cave?
What scaffold props my roof,
curves out damp walls,
all velvet-hung?
Moist flesh,
indenting to my touch,
closes like giant clam,
a curling tongue.
Some swallowed, mucus-tacky fish
noses its scaly length about my neck,
lost in the slap of falling sea.
Salt rinses mouth and lips
and all around the stench
of half-digested fish
breathes over me.

JUDITH NICHOLLS

JOHN, JOHN THE BAPTIST

John, John the Baptist
Lived in a desert of stone,
He had no money,
Ate beans and honey,
And he lived quite on his own.

His coat was made of camel,
His belt was made of leather,
And deep in the gleam
Of a twisting stream
He'd stand in every weather.

John, John the Baptist,
Worked without any pay,
But he'd hold your hand
And bring you to land
And wash your fears away.

CHARLES CAUSLEY

SHEEP AND LAMBS

All in the April evening,
April airs were abroad,
The sheep with their little lambs
Passed me by on the road.

The sheep with their little lambs
Passed me by on the road;
All in the April evening
I thought on the Lamb of God.

The lambs were weary and crying
With a weak, human cry.
I thought on the Lamb of God
Going meekly to die.

Up in the blue, blue mountains
Dewy pastures are sweet;
Rest for the little bodies,
Rest for the little feet.

But for the Lamb of God,
Up on the hill-top green,
Only a cross of shame
Two stark crosses between.

All in the April evening,
April airs were abroad,
I saw the sheep with their lambs,
And thought on the Lamb of God.

KATHARINE TYNAN

ONCE UPON A TIME

Once upon a time there lived a man who was a miracle,
Once upon a time there grew a man like God;
All the people came to him to listen to his teaching,
Children gladdened at his touch, and men grew good.

Blind girls blinked their eyes awake and saw the world
    all coloured;
Crooked men stood straight as trees, alive and strong;
Lonely people lifted up their hearts like flowers
    to sunshine,
Crippled children danced for joy, and dumb boys sang.

Always I am with you, said this man who was a miracle,
I will never leave you till the seas run dry;
Listen for me, look for me, and you will surely find me;
And the wonder of my touch will bring you joy.

M.E. ROSE

Feasts and Festivals

A BRIGHT STAR SHONE

A
star
shines
I
am a
fir tree.
Each year at
Christmas, dads come
and buy me.
Children hang bright
baubles, for ev'ryone to see.
Beneath my branches,
piled untidily, gifts in bright
wrappers,
wait for days to be
opened. On that day, a little baby
was born, in a stable, to gentle Mary. There
in Bethlehem, King David's
city. A manger bed was all there seemed to be,
oxen and asses, standing so quietly, worshipped God's dear son
with Joseph's grey donkey
for
this
baby
king
Angels sang sweetly, and a bright
star shone. So sing carols softly,
ev'ry Christmastide

JANIS PRIESTLEY

CHRISTMAS TREE

Gold was among the gifts
that the wise men brought to Jesus.
(See how the tall one lifts

the sack from his saddle
and pours the coins into the lap
of Mary by the cradle?)

Gold is a gift for kings;
but wise men aren't the only ones
who understand such things.

For on the western side
of Australia, a peculiar tree
fills the bush with pride

each Christmas, with a bold
and brilliant display of blossoms
as bright as molten gold.

Rejoice! Even the odd,
the unlovely and misshapen
may offer gifts to God!

Christmas trees are ugly
trees. Their leaves are tatty and dull
and their limbs are straggly.

Their wood's a carpenter's loss,
being too weak to bear the weight
of a rafter or a cross.

And yet on Christmas Day,
between banksias and eucalypts,
by roads and in paddocks, they

blaze with a beauty that hurts
the eye. (See them fling their nuggets
into the sky's blue skirts!)

Nuytsia floribunda:
a little tree with gifts of gold
on the Day of Wonder!

ANDREW LANSDOWN

71

CHRISTMAS DAYBREAK

Before the paling of the stars,
Before the winter morn,
Before the earliest cockcrow,
Jesus Christ was born:
Born in a stable,
Cradled in a manger,
In the world His hands had made,
Born a stranger.

Priest and king lay fast asleep
In Jerusalem,
Young and old lay fast asleep
In crowded Bethlehem:
Saint and angel, ox and ass,
Kept a watch together,
Before the Christmas daybreak
In the winter weather.

Jesus on His Mother's breast
In the stable cold,
Spotless Lamb of God was He,
Shepherd of the fold.
Let us kneel with Mary Maid,
With Joseph bent and hoary,*
With saint and angel, ox and ass,
To hail the King of Glory.

CHRISTINA ROSSETTI

* hoary = grey-haired with age

CHRISTMAS MORN

Shall I tell you what will come
to Bethlehem on Christmas morn,
who will kneel them gently down
before the Lord new-born?

One small fish from the river,
with scales of red, red gold,
one wild bee from the heather,
one grey lamb from the fold,
one ox from the high pasture,
one black bull from the herd,
one goatling from the far hills,
one white, white bird.

And many children—God give them grace,
bringing tall candles to light Mary's face.

RUTH SAWYER

THE BARN

'I am tired of this barn!' said the colt.
'And every day it snows.
Outside there's no grass any more
And icicles grow on my nose.
I am tired of hearing the cows
Breathing and talking together.
I am sick of these clucking hens.
I *hate* stables and winter weather!'

'Hush, little colt,' said the mare
'And a story I will tell
Of a barn like this one of ours
And the wonders that there befell.
It was weather much like this,
And the beasts stood as we stand now
In the warm good dark of the barn—
A horse and an ass and a cow.'

'And sheep?' asked the colt. 'Yes, sheep,
And a pig and a goat and a hen.
All of the beasts of the barnyard,
The usual servants of men.
And into their midst came a lady
And she was cold as death,
But the animals leaned above her
And made her warm with their breath.

'There was her baby born
And laid to sleep in the hay,
While music flooded the rafters
And the barn was as light as day.
And angels and kings and shepherds
Came to worship the babe from afar,
But we looked at him first of all creatures
By the bright strange light of a star!'

ELIZABETH COATSWORTH

WHAT THE DONKEY SAW

No room in the inn, of course,
And not that much in the stable,
What with the shepherds, Magi, Mary,
Joseph, the heavenly host—
Not to mention the baby
Using our manger as a cot.
You couldn't have squeezed another cherub in
For love or money.

Still, in spite of the overcrowding,
I did my best to make them feel wanted.
I could see that the baby and I
Would be going places together.

U.A. FANTHORPE

CAROL

Mary laid her Child among
The bracken-fronds of night—
And by the glimmer round His head
All the barn was lit.

Mary held her Child above
The miry, frozen farm—
And by the fire within His limbs
The resting roots were warm.

Mary hid her Child between
Hillocks of hard sand—
By singing water in His veins
Grass sprang from the ground.

Mary nursed her Child beside
The gardens of a grave—
And by the death within His bones
The dead became alive.

NORMAN NICHOLSON

CHESTER CAROL

He who made the earth so fair
Slumbers in a stable bare,
Warmed by cattle standing there.

Oxen, lowing stand all round;
In the stall no other sound.
Mars the peace by Mary found.

Joseph piles the soft, sweet hay,
Starlight drives the dark away,
Angels sing a heavenly lay.

Jesus sleeps in Mary's arm
Sheltered there from rude alarm,
None can do Him ill or harm.

See His mother o'er Him bend
Hers the joy to soothe and tend,
Hers the bliss that knows no end.

CHESTER MYSTERY PLAY

A CHRISTMAS CAROL

The Christ-child lay on Mary's lap,
His hair was like a light.
(O weary, weary were the world,
But here is all aright.)

The Christ-child lay on Mary's breast,
His hair was like a star.
(O stern and cunning are the kings,
But here the true hearts are.)

The Christ-child lay on Mary's heart,
His hair was like a fire.
(O weary, weary is the world,
But here the world's desire.)

The Christ-child stood at Mary's knee,
His hair was like a crown,
And all the flowers looked up at him,
And all the stars looked down.

G.K. CHESTERTON

77

THE SHEPHERDS' CAROL

We stood on the hills, Lady,
Our day's work done,
Watching the frosted meadows
That winter had won.

The evening was calm, Lady,
The air so still,
Silence more lovely than music
Folded the hill.

There was a star, Lady,
Shone in the night,
Larger than Venus it was
And bright, so bright.

Oh, a voice from the sky, Lady,
It seemed to us then
Telling of God being born
In the world of men.

And so we have come, Lady,
Our day's work done,
Our love, our hopes, ourselves
We give to your son.

CLIVE SANSOM

KINGS CAME RIDING

Kings came riding
One, two, and three,
Over the desert
And over the sea.

One in a ship
With a silver mast;
The fishermen wondered
As he went past.

One on a horse
With a saddle of gold;
The children came running
To behold.

One came walking,
Over the sand,
With a casket of treasure
Held in his hand.

All the people
Said, 'Where go they?'
But the kings went forward
All through the day.

Night came on
As those kings went by:
They shone like the gleaming
Stars in the sky.

CHARLES WILLIAMS

CAROL OF THE BROWN KING

Of the three Wise Men
Who came to the King,
One was a brown man,
So they sing.

Of the three Wise Men
Who followed the Star,
One was a brown king
From afar.

They brought fine gifts
Of spices and gold
In jewelled boxes
Of beauty untold.

Unto His humble
Manger they came
And bowed their heads
In Jesus' name.

Three Wise Men,
One dark like me—
Part of His
Nativity.

LANGSTON HUGHES

POEM FOR EASTER

Tell me:
What came first
Easter or the egg?
Crucifixion
      or daffodils?
Three days in a tomb
      or four days
in Paris?
      (returning
Bank Holiday Monday).

When is a door
not a door?
When it is rolled away.
When is a body
not a body?
When it is risen.

Question.
Why was it the Saviour
rode on the cross?
Answer.
To get us
to the other side.

Behold I stand.
Behold I stand and what?
Behold I stand at the door and

knock knock.

STEVE TURNER

EASTER EGGS

Easter eggs! Easter eggs! Give to him that begs!
For Christ the Lord is arisen.

To the poor, open door, something give from your store!
For Christ the Lord is arisen.

Those who hoard can't afford, moth and rust their reward!
For Christ the Lord is arisen

Eastertide, like a bride, comes, and won't be denied.
For Christ the Lord is arisen

ANON (TRANSLATED FROM A TRADITIONAL RUSSIAN EASTER SONG)

HARVEST POEM

Fruit and nuts and berries,
Growing ripe and sweet,
Vegetables and golden corn
All for us to eat.

Rich food in its plenty,
Picked and stored away,
While others in their countries
Are starving every day.

Mothers in the market,
Choosing what to eat,
Perhaps a rich fruit pudding
For a special treat.

In heats of Ethiopia,
Little grows on land.
A mother looks at the food for the day
Which only fills one hand.

In lands of drought and hunger
No more, dear Lord, we pray
Will mothers ask the question
Which child to feed today?

JAMES ANTHONY CAREY (AGED 10)

PLANTING THE SEEDS

Here is the seed going into the ground
That grows into wheat yellow and round
That is threshed by combined harvester power
That is ground between stones to make fine flour
That is mixed into dough with water and yeast
That is cooked into bread for our daily feast
Which reminds us of Christ the body of life.

Here is the seed going into the ground
That grows into grapes red and round
That is squashed in a press to get juice from the flesh
That is poured into vats while it is still fresh
That is mixed with water, sugar and yeast
That is stored in green bottles for a family feast
Which reminds us of Christ the blood of life.

STEVE STICKLEY

Whispering in God's Ear

MORNING PRAYER

Now another day is breaking,
Sleep was sweet and so is waking,
Dear Lord I promised you last night
Never again to sulk or fight.
Such vows are easier to keep
When a child is sound asleep.
Today, O Lord, for your dear sake,
I'll try to keep them when awake.

OGDEN NASH

DAYBREAK

The moon shines bright,
The stars give light
Before the break of day;
God bless you all
Both great and small
And send you a joyful day.

TRADITIONAL

GOD BLESS THE FIELD

God bless the field and bless the furrow
Stream and branch and rabbit burrow,
Hill and stone and flower and tree,
From Bristol town to Wetherby—
Bless the sun and bless the sleet,
Bless the lane and bless the street,
Bless the night and bless the day,
From Somerset and all the way
To the meadows of Cathay;
Bless the minnow, bless the whale,
Bless the rainbow and the hail,
Bless the nest and bless the leaf,
Bless the righteous and the thief,
Bless the wing and bless the fin,
Bless the air I travel in,
Bless the mill and bless the mouse,
Bless the miller's bricken house,
Bless the earth and bless the sea,
God bless you and God bless me.

ANON

BRIGHT MORNIN' STARS

Bright mornin' stars are risin'
Bright mornin' stars are risin'
Bright mornin' stars are risin'
Day is a-breakin' in my soul.

Oh where are our dear fathers?
Oh where are our dear mothers?
Oh where are sisters and brothers?
Day is a-breakin' in my soul.

Some are down in the valley prayin',
Some are deep in the mountain sleepin',
Some are up in heaven shoutin',
Day is a-breakin' in my soul.

TRADITIONAL APPALACHIAN HYMN

OUT IN THE FIELDS WITH GOD

The little cares that fretted me,
I lost them yesterday,
Among the fields above the sea,
Among the winds at play,
Among the lowing of the herds,
The rustling of the trees,
Among the singing of the birds,
The humming of the bees.

The foolish fears of what might pass
I cast them all away
Among the clover-scented grass
Among the new-mown hay,
Among the hushing of the corn
Where drowsy poppies nod,
Where ill thoughts die and good are born—
Out in the fields with God.

LOUISE IMOGEN GUINEY

SMALL THINGS

Dear Father
hear and bless
Thy beasts and singing birds:
And guard
with tenderness
small things
that have no words.

ANON

ONLY A FOOL

Only a fool would fail
To praise God in his might
When the tiny mindless birds
Praise him in their flight.

ANON (TRANSLATED FROM THE IRISH BY BRENDAN KENNELLY)

PRAYER OF A FISHERMAN

Lord let me catch a fish
So large that even I,
In telling of it afterwards,
Shall have no need to lie.

ANON

THE PRAYER OF THE LITTLE DUCKS

Dear God,
Give us a flood of water.
Let it rain tomorrow and always.
Give us plenty of little slugs
And other luscious things to eat.
Protect all folk who·quack
And everyone who knows how to swim.
Amen

CARMEN BERNOS DE GASZTOLD (TRANSLATED BY RUMER GODDEN)

A CHILD'S GRACE

Here a little child I stand
Heaving up my either hand
Cold as paddocks* though they be,
Here I lift them up to thee,
For a benison* to fall
On our meat, and on us all.

ROBERT HERRICK

WATER-ICES

For water-ices, cheap but good,
That find us in a thirsty mood;
For ices made of milk or cream
That slip down smoothly as a dream;
For cornets, sandwiches and pies
That make the gastric juices rise;
For ices bought in little shops
Or at the kerb from him who stops;
For chanting of the sweet refrain:
'Vanilla, strawberry or plain?'
We thank Thee, Lord, who sendst with heat
This cool deliciousness to eat.

ALLEN M. LAING

* paddocks = toads, benison = blessing

EVENING

in words of one syllable

The day is past, the sun is set,
And the white stars are in the sky;
While the long grass with dew is wet,
And through the air the bats now fly.

The lambs have now lain down to sleep,
The birds have long since sought their nests;
The air is still; and dark, and deep
On the hill side the old wood rests.

Yet of the dark I have no fear,
But feel as safe as when 'tis light;
For I know God is with me there,
And he will guard me through the night.

For God is by me when I pray,
And when I close mine eyes in sleep,
I know that he will with me stay,
And will all night watch by me keep.

For he who rules the stars and sea,
Who makes the grass and trees to grow,
Will look on a poor child like me,
When on my knees I to him bow.

He holds all things in his right hand,
The rich, the poor, the great, the small,
When we sleep, or sit, or stand,
Is with us, for he loves us all.

THOMAS MILLER

AFRICAN LULLABY

Sleep my little one! The night is all wind and rain;
The meal has been wet by the raindrops
   and bent is the sugar cane;
O Giver who gives to the people,
   in safety my little son keep!
My little son with the head-dress, sleep, sleep, sleep!

TRADITIONAL EAST AFRICAN (TRANSLATED BY HOLLING C. HOLLING)

HOLY LULLABY

Sleep, baby, sleep.
Thy father guards the sheep;
Thy mother shakes the dreamland tree,
Down falls a little dream for thee:
Sleep, baby, sleep.

Sleep, baby, sleep.
The large stars are the sheep;
The little stars are the lambs, I guess;
And the gentle moon is the shepherdess:
Sleep, baby, sleep.

Sleep, baby, sleep.
Our Saviour loves His sheep;
He is the Lamb of God on high,
Who for our sakes came down to die:
Sleep, baby, sleep.

ANON

GHOULIES AND GHOSTIES

From ghoulies and ghosties
Long leggety beasties
And things that go bump in the night
Good Lord deliver us.

TRADITIONAL CORNISH

GERMAN SLUMBER SONG

Go to sleep and good night;
In a rosy twilight,
With the moon overhead
Snuggle deep in your bed.
God will watch, never fear,
While Heaven draws near.

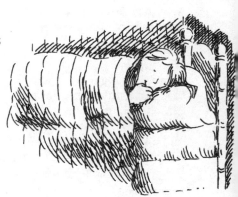

Go to sleep and good night;
You are safe in the sight
Of the angels who show
Christmas trees all aglow.
So to sleep, shut your eyes,
In a dream's Paradise.

KARL SIMROCK (ADAPTED BY LOUIS UNTERMEYER)

A BLESSING

God bless all those that I love;
God bless all those that love me;
God bless all those that love those that I love,
All those that love those that love me.

A NEW ENGLAND SAMPLER

GOING TO HEAVEN!

Going to Heaven!
I don't know when—
Pray do not ask me how!
Indeed, I'm too astonished
To think of answering you!
Going to Heaven!
How dim it sounds!
And yet it will be done
As sure as flocks go home at night
Unto the Shepherd's arm!

Perhaps you're going too!
Who knows?
If you should get there first
Save just a little space for me
Close to the two I lost—
The smallest 'Robe' will fit me
And just a bit of 'Crown'—
For you know we do not mind our dress
When we are going home—

EMILY DICKINSON

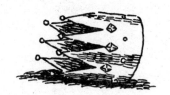

UPHILL

Does the road wind uphill all the way?
Yes, to the very end.
Will the day's journey take the whole long day?
From morn to night, my friend.

But is there for the night a resting-place?
A roof for when the slow, dark hours begin.
May not the darkness hide it from my face?
You cannot miss that inn.

Shall I meet other wayfarers at night?
Those who have gone before.
Then must I knock, or call when just in sight?
They will not keep you standing at that door.

Shall I find comfort, travel-sore and weak?
Of labour you shall find the sum.
Will there be beds for me and all who seek?
Yea, beds for all who come.

CHRISTINA ROSSETTI

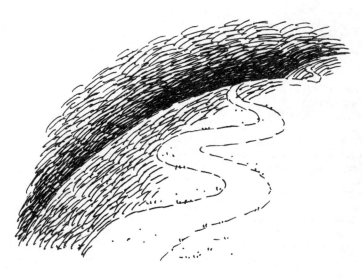

Subject index

Index of first lines

Acknowledgments

Thanks go to all those who have given permission to include poems in this book, as indicated in the list below. Every effort has been made to trace and contact copyright owners. If there are any inadvertent omissions or errors in the acknowledgments, we apologize to those concerned and will remedy these in the next edition.

The National Exhibition of Children's Art, for 'Harvest Poem', by James Anthony Carey

Reprinted by permission of David Higham Associates: 'Here's the Reverend Rundle' and 'John, John the Baptist' from *Early in the Morning* published by Viking Penguin; Eleanor Farjeon, 'Cat' from *Silver, Sand and Snow* published by Michael Joseph; 'Fred' from *The Children's Bells* published by Oxford University Press

'The Long Giraffe' from the collection *A Giant's Scrapbook* by Stewart Henderson, copyright © 1989, published by Hodder & Stoughton

'cHILD pRODIGY' from the collection *Homeland* by Stewart Henderson, copyright © 1993, published by Hodder & Stoughton

Alfred A. Knopf for 'Heaven' by Langston Hughes from *Selected Poems* copyright © 1947 Langston Hughes

Estate of Langston Hughes for 'Carol of the Brown King' by Langston Hughes

Elizabeth Jennings for her poems 'Friends' and 'The Clown' published by Macmillan Publishers Ltd, and for 'Spell of the Earth'

Allen M. Laing for 'For Water-Ices' from *Prayers and Graces*. All our attempts at tracing the copyright holder were unsuccessful.

Andrew Lansdown for his poems 'Frightening Father' and 'Christmas Tree'

'My Bath' by Madeleine L'Engle. Copyright © 1974 by Crosswicks Ltd. This usage granted by permission.

Fount/HarperCollins for 'The Dragon Speaks' from *Poems* by C.S. Lewis

George MacBeth for his poem 'Rain'

'Giving Thanks Giving Thanks', from *Fresh Paint* by Eve Merriam. Copyright © 1986 Eve Merriam. Reprinted by permission of Marian Reiner

Millie Murray for her poem 'Spare Rib'

Curtis Brown Ltd for 'Morning Prayer' by Ogden Nash

Faber & Faber Ltd for 'Jonah's Lament' and 'David and Goliath' by Judith Nicholls

Reprinted by permission of David Higham Associates: 'Carol' by Norman Nicholson from *Five Rivers*

Adrian Plass for his poem 'Winter Walk' from *Clearing Away the Rubbish*, published by Minstrel/Monarch

Janis Priestley for 'A Bright Star Shone'

Collins/HarperCollins for 'Once Upon a Time' by M.E. Rose from *The Golden Cockerel Book of Morning Readings*

Reprinted by permission of David Higham Associates Limited: 'The Shepherds' Carol' by Clive Sansom from *The Witnesses and Other Poems* by Clive Sansom. Published by Methuen

Viking Penguin, Inc. for 'Christmas Morn' from *The Long Christmas* by Ruth Sawyer

Mike Starkey for 'Not Like Us'

Steve Stickley for 'Planting the Seeds'

J.M. Dent & Sons for 'The Smile' from *Collected Poems 1945–90* by R.S. Thomas

Allen & Unwin/HarperCollins for 'Cat' from *The Adventures of Tom Bombadil* by J.R.R. Tolkien

Steve Turner for 'Poem for Easter' from *Up To Date* and 'The Naming of the Animals' from *The Day I Fell Down the Toilet and Other Poems*

Louis Untermeyer for 'Questions at Night' from *Rainbow in the Sky*